The Moon

Written by Tracey Michele

Picture Dictionary

crater

full moon

spacesuit

surface

telescope

When you look into the sky
at night, you can see the moon.
The moon is a big ball of rock
in the sky.
It does not have its own light.
It gets its light from the sun.

The moon looks bigger
than the stars in the sky.

A man called Galileo
looked at the moon
through a telescope.
A telescope is a tool.
It makes faraway things
look closer.
It makes them look bigger.
You can see the moon clearly
with a telescope.

This is a picture of Galileo looking through his telescope.

The moon
is about four times smaller
than Earth.
The surface of the moon
is rocky and dusty.
There are mountains and craters
on the moon's surface.

Moon craters are large holes.

Weather on the Moon

The moon's weather
is not like Earth's weather.
There is no wind or rain
on the moon.
It can be very hot.
The temperature can be 100°C
in the daytime.
It can be very cold.
The temperature can be -170°C
at night.

Temperatures on the Moon

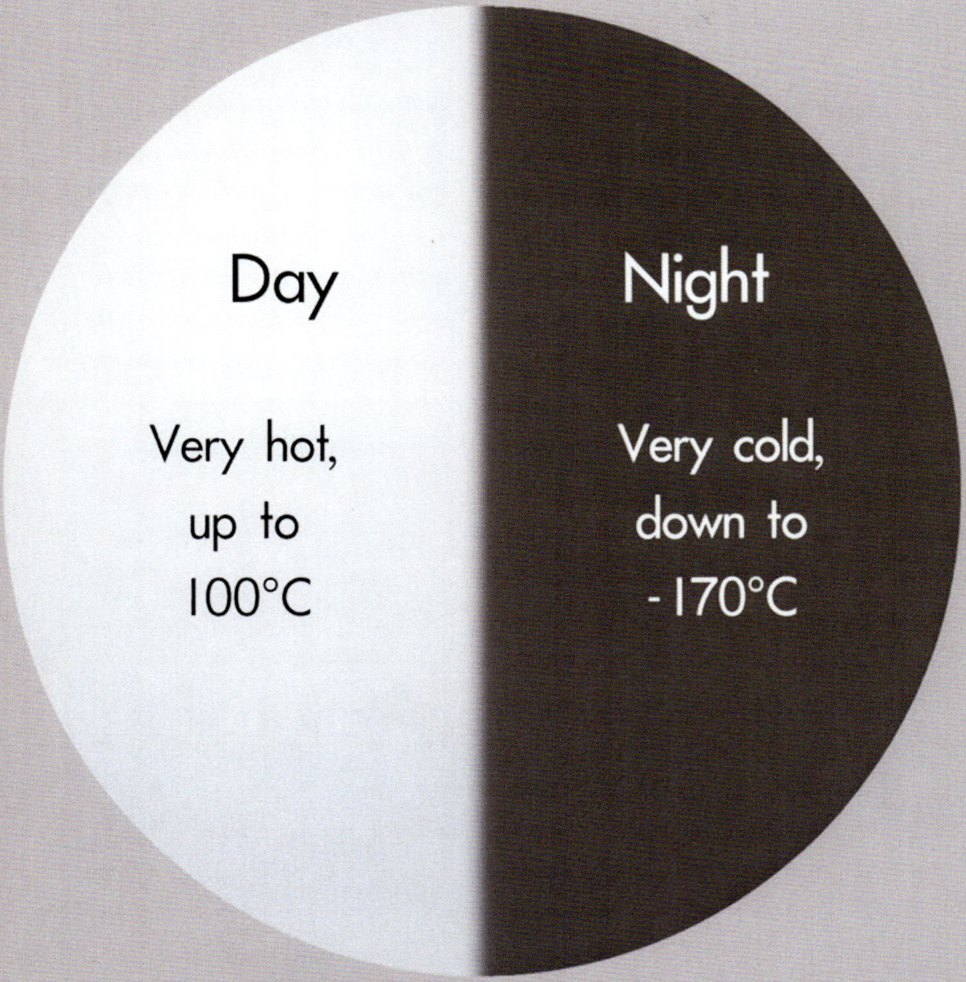

The Phases of the Moon

The moon moves around Earth.
It takes the moon about 28 days
to move around Earth.
The moon seems to change shape
as it moves around Earth.
Some nights you can see
the full moon.
Some nights you can see half
of the moon.
Some nights you cannot see
the moon at all.

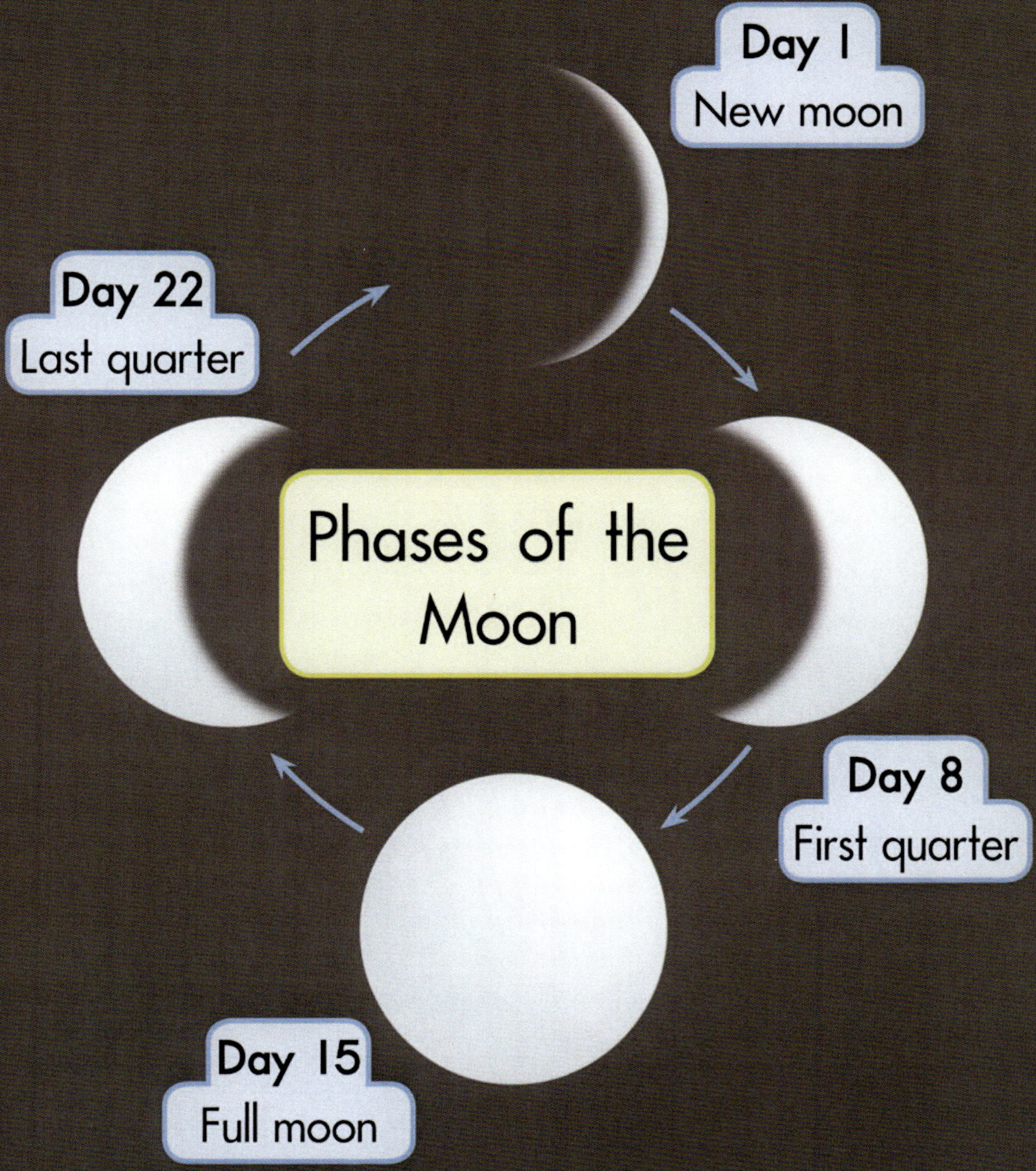
Day 1
New moon
Day 22
Last quarter
Phases of the Moon
Day 8
First quarter
Day 15
Full moon

Travel to the Moon

The first man
to walk on the moon
was Neil Armstrong.
He went to the moon
in a spaceship called *Apollo 11*.
He wore a spacesuit.
He landed on the moon
on July 20, 1969.

This astronaut is stepping down onto the moon.

Neil Armstrong did big jumps
on the moon.
He could jump high
because the moon does not have
much gravity.
Gravity is the force
that pulls things down
to the ground.

This astronaut carries air to breathe on the moon.

Activity Page

1. Keep track of the moon.
2. Go outside every night for one month.
3. Look at the moon.
4. Draw what you see.
5. Write the date on your picture.
6. Write if it is a full moon or a quarter moon.

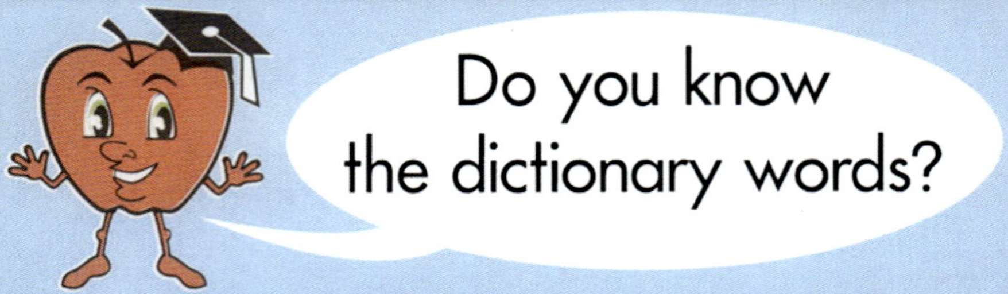